LOOSE SUGAR

WESLEYAN POETRY

LOOSE SUGAR

Brenda Hillman

Wesleyan University Press

Published by University Press of New England
Hanover and London

Wesleyan University Press
Published by University Press of New England, Hanover, NH 03755
© 1997 by Brenda Hillman
Printed in the United States of America
5 4 3 2
CIP data appear at the end of the book

The publisher gratefully acknowledges the support of Lannan Foundation
in the publication of this book.

For Ethan, Jesse, and Louisa

CONTENTS

LOOSE SUGAR

I

space
_____
time

space-time:

> *The four-dimensional space*
> *whose points are events.*

Stephen Hawking
  glossary for *A Brief History of Time*

And what you see outside of you
 you see inside of you . . .

"The Thunder: Perfect Mind"
Nag Hammadi Library

The Spark

Once you were immortal in the flame.
You were not the fire
but you were in the fire;—

nothing moved except
the way it was already moving;
nothing spoke
except the voice in back of time;—

and when you became your life,
there were those who couldn't,
those who tried to love you and failed
and some who had loved you in the beginning
with the first sexual energy of the world.

Start the memory now,
you who let your life be invented
though not being invented had been more available

and remember those
who lit the abyss. The boys in science fair.
You were probably hall monitor at that time weren't you,
and you admired them;
on their generator, the spark bounced back and forth
like baby lightning
and you saw them run their fingertips
through its danger,
two promising loops stuck up to provide
a home for the sexual light
which was always loose when it wasn't broken,
free joy that didn't go anywhere
but moved between the wires
like a piece of living, in advance—

then later: how much
were you supposed to share?

The boys sat in front of your house at dusk,
the ones who still had parents.
Sometimes they held Marlboros out the car
windows and even
if they didn't, sparks fell from their hands.
Showers of sparks
between nineteen sixty eight and the

hands were sleek
with asking sleek with asking;—

they had those long intramural after
the library type fingers
they would later put in you,—ah.
When? well,
when they had talked you into having a body
they could ask into the depths of

and they rose to meet you
against an ignorance that made you perfect
and you rose to meet them like a waitress of fire—

because: didn't
the spark shine best in the bodies
under the mild shooting stars
on the back-and-forth blanket
from the fathers' cars—
they lay down with you, and when
did you start missing them.
As Sacramento missed its yellow dust 1852.
When did you start missing those
who invented your body with their sparks—

they didn't mind being
plural. They put
their summer stars inside of you,

how nice to have. And then:
the pretty soon. Pretty
soon you were a body,

4

space, warm
flesh, warm
(this) under
the summer meteors that fell
like lower case i's above
the cave of granite where the white owl slept

without because or why
that first evening of the world. The sparks
of your bodies joined the loud sparks of the sky—

And you carried it, a little flame,
into almost famous cities,
between the ringing of shallow bells,
pretty much like some of that
blue tile work,
walking the bridge of sighs until you found the spark

on quilted bedspreads
in small villages, as if
the not-mattering stitching coming
all 'undone' in the middle
stood for a decade. You barely
burned then;

sex grows rather dim sometimes
doesn't it but it comes back.
Yourself half-gone into those rooms, yourself, a stranger.

You who happened only once:
remember yourself as you are;

when he comes to you
in the revolving dusk,
his full self lighting candles, a little smoke
he sings, the fire
you already own so you can stop
not letting him;

all love is representative

of the beginning of time. When you are loved,
the darkness carries you.
When you are loved, you are golden—

(that's good, you got there;
  should you make it
part of the record?)

Thicket Group

. . . a burning liquid that was called the original force of Nature

—anonymous tenth-century alchemist

A Power

For some reason it's likely to think of the insides of a thicket
        as a five-pointed liquid star.

A group of us, not knowing how to stand in nature, in the
        sixties; each breath sponsored by that.

Possible friends nearby smelled like hemp, white tortillas
        and twelve-oz. Coca-Colas; the fire in their fingers
        talked back, had feelings.

Locating consciousness, where would you say it is;
        "it was the happiest moment in the first twenty years."

And, why do we seek to destroy it by changing?

mottled doves

garnets

Empty Spines

Magic fought with the ideal, time
        curved the barren glow, and animals called from their
        nests at the center of the world.

I had been a child being guessed at by onyx, fresh
        from nothing. Dimension's pawn.

My brother okayed the ground with sticks; when
        something called, we answered it. With a drop or two
        more of that inherited chemical we would have been
        a schizophrenic.

Empty spines of sticks filled up with liquid fire; they had done this
        before, we just hadn't been quiet enough to mention it.

 Making theories of creation is about repetition, though even
        the infinite happens just once.

XX sticks
cross-referencing
each other

9

A Window

Had intended to climb out a window, but intended is not
        what makes it happen. Delicious to climb out a window.
        The weather was not the window's fault.

Smears on chrome fenders like pet clouds between which
        they might see a body coming curved to them. Before
        the thicket your mouth stopped off at a boy.

Going back a little: nearing them was faster; that which
        owned the thicket also owned the flower.

Either tell the story or don't. Narrative is such an either/or
        situation, like a window, just as sex is a metaphor for
        not getting it.

You have changed the assignment to Swirl: voice from
        a thicket; surfaces meet where you live into things.
        A body is a place missed specifically. They met you
        in your body, where you couldn't go alone.

The spell:
    unable
    unable
    unable
    pretty soon

The Thicket

A power came up; it was in between the voices.
        It said you could stop making sense.

Have you seen it? Of course you have. Based on
        what? A red bird that caught fire on the alchemist's
        table.

The girls stood around in long paisley dresses, coyote cries
        coming through them, something frightened and
        being canceled. We weren't on drugs then.
        The thicket looked like a star of pub(l)ic hair.

You always want to control how everything will turn out,
        is the problem.

Suburban kids—on the edge of change—give up hope of being
        understood. Why did the fire need to rest in us after
        that fluttery little absolute terror of childhood.

(wands being

on fire)

Dust Devils

A power came up. It flew toward the guessing Cloud.
        It was not as curved as night or straight as day.

Have you heard it? Of course you have. It settled in the
        lyndon-johnson desert, supervising funnels,
        eisenhower-bird-egg-head, stomach of peace and battles.

Standing before the thicket in long clothes not having sex. In the
        bible, you can't worship fire without worshipping dust,
        and whether you *fought* depression had everything to do
        with this.

A fire undaunted by the place where the years live.

To be patient with the kind of plot in which nothing happens,
        alchemists devised a burning water that didn't wet
        the hands. Elements mixed, swirled together, became
        decorative. Art comes from loneliness.

The Arroyo

—The perspective of lines or

innocence—

I love other bodies.

They always seemed to know
the secret before I did . . .

My mother has come outside to hang up towels: Cannon.
      I'm in my nada body, I'm about ten
      dragging magnets through sand
      in the arroyo to collect garnets from iron filings . . .

For others, it's "the ditch" or "the wash" or "drainage ditch"—

she's the thin expert at hanging out daily life. Squinting, I see
she's either a 1
or a 0 who never makes a mistake outdoors . . . pink towels, shorts,
sock sock / sock sock . . . The sun is the mistake that works.

The dragging then the filings then picking out
      garnets with tweezers in the 100 degree
      heat of the arroyo—

She calls my name;
it brightens; it's years before my period: chrome
glint of the abandoned fender; the doll's head
softens near the jar. These garnets
have backward facets. The present tense saddens them. Before
the flash flood I can make it
to the end of the arroyo where the hollow
chalk couple has been shown having sex on a rock.

If knowing alternates with seeing,

dragging magnets through the sand thinking of them
is the place where I am not.

Childhood is one of our low points.

When I cough, the doves
        fly away . . .
She hangs up clothes
        her single, her nada humming, when she
        turns sideways she is gone. Pinch bird-beak
        clothespins. She uses my whole name to call me in—)

A power comes up, it's in between the voices, it says
        you can stop making sense . . .

The hollow chalk couple—
        oh when I see them   I will touch their penis;

it is the small blue tombstone turned sideways.

Touching it is the invention of the new. Touching
the signs next to them—FUCK DICK   (heart heart heart)
is the both invention. Sex and more
exciting than doing it without talking—

>   *I looked for the one who sought me*
>   *without measure and the waters broke away . . .*
>   *Waited for one who called*
>   *but she had gone in. I called*
>   *my love much later   the same*
>   *when I was not him.*

The doll has become soft when left
for about twenty minutes; white   *s   take over the eyes;
our garnets on wax paper like menstrual blood.

Floods will come over the earth
but the hollow's better; winds replace

the chalk couple with sand;
the hawk sweeps and is gone; coyote; various
night viceroys with yellow eyes;
Hollow body fills later (in legs
with) specks of time,
boys with wandering and orderly hands; laughter; such as— oh D.
        oh P., oh L., oh P., and oh A.

I loved other bodies.   Even those
I did not love   (those of this generation, we all . . .)

Cruel lovers and kind, when stoned in the south
and beaches between . . . And the faceless
chalk couple haunts me now: taught: touch
language with the north hand, flesh
with the right;

even three decades later, in danger
of sort of, the new disease and terror
of backward,
convinced one self is not
the way to live because we are lived *through*—

not to fail what was left blank—

I gather the little jars of the elements,
                            to show her;

within pure joy exists
a kind of hollow,
the inverse river, the opposite water—

Early Sex

The one-celled creature brought to class
in the drop of pond water
took its main hunger around on the slide,

it had yes for a skin and a thousand
little hairs for feet
to help it decide . . . You wanted to love the others

no matter what,
swam over the edge of yourself, swam
in the place that seemed like forever,

you loved when they visited you,
you changed shape for them and when they left
you were the same as water

It's just that it's not quite time
to write them . . . What
shall I do while I'm waiting.
—Wait harder, it said.

Orion's Belt

Read this by your own light,
little body;
read this with your eyes closed;

under the three stars
you learned the origins of love.

When they took you out,
you would push the buttons of their jeans
with your thumb

and the stars stretched in Orion's belt
like the three mysteries
at the start of time.

Dentyne and dope
on their breath—mostly Dentyne.
Long warm breath

between watching spaces, between
the light that left Orion
a million years ago,   and they

tried to see no body
up there, no guilty party,

but to speak of the forces
that made them: hydrogen, helium,
like legendary women,

and at the edge of the universe,
a little buzzing—like a phone left off the hook . . .

They lay on the hoods of cars
(warm engine: ticking) and you
undid their belts;—

Orion lay on his right side,
then on his left, his belt
undone, the three stars

doomed to circle
like the three mysteries at the start of time:

why it happened,
why we suffer,
and how love bothers at all . . .

When you think of those
you will not touch again
in this lifetime

you own a few points on the one body.
Some made you happy.
Everything else—

the pale sword of the hunter,
the uplifted sandal,

everything else mostly fades
in the folds of heaven—

Active Magic

You want to know where you are again?
Back in the middle of the interrupted everything
third side of the double album,
the start of the night shift
as eternity's waitress;
it's dusk, many years after the war,
you've crossed the same wild fields as before;
they've started selling uniforms of new dead soldiers,
gone back to putting peace signs on t-shirts—;
you're stepping lightly in the dream
you can afford, the magic that was
and always must have been for you—

A dusk ago,—Remember?   don't you.
Remember? Look. You had
an old soul. Killdeer
landed in the fields out there,
landed in their sounds,
in what's already happening,
dee, d-dee,
near your dormitory room,
you stretched once like an oak tree,
many times like a laurel;
the ones who would be drafted
came into your room

and you had an old soul.
You had started the same soul
five times, you were good at it;
the moon watched you one of those times
peering in at you
before you had lain down, peered in
behind the loaded cypress;
the moon horizoned herself,
you told her your sexual secrets,
loved what she could not help

being farther then—

The ones who would be drafted
came into the room (it's still possible,
the never happening); you thought
you'd been sent to earth to rescue them,
said, leave them alone, they already have tenses;
they draped blue workshirts over chairs—;
the moon was doing her moon imitation,
old waitress, tilting herself like a tray,
said to the war, leave them alone,
they have what they want,
they don't need a future
when they have a soul . . . And why

shouldn't they have. (Headlights
shattered them. Loud
white damage of oncoming cars.)
You thought you'd been sent to earth
to help them not to fight—
when they rained with the rain,
when they clouded,
they were the little bit almost,
a little bit Sacramento, in love
with the magic of the active ground,
and you rode north or south with them,
on the backs of Triumphs, in the vans—

You afraid? Not really.
You afraid? Not really no.   OK OK
if you get afraid just tell me—
till you stopped in the middle of orchards
with little hard crosses, in love
with the magic of the active ground;
why, every seed moved!
Shook and shook.
Even the necklacey Woolworth's ones
the spiders loved—and why
shouldn't they have. Night
was coming on—

it was dusk
between the stages of the war. You
would save them. Dusk lifted you
with 2 fingers like a field mouse
and set you down 2 hawks from here
where you had done the other game,
pawn to queen four, the being
active till you loved
the mind and body of their world,
and lay in the low thin dormitory
boats of those beds of theirs,
their noisy hands all over you—;

you know how mercury shakes?
You know how mercury shivers
like tomorrow when you break
the end off the thermometer?
You see your own face in the silver.
Active magic. You could
become like that.
They gave you a body
before they left, made love to you
so easily it felt like spending money;
after the marching and the shouting
they left the voices in your flesh . . .

Some of them got free. Some left. Some died.
One fought the war in you.
When they rained with the rain,
when they clouded, in eaches
and whens, the water streaming
from their bodies as they left,
when their faces lay,
when your mouth lay, when their
mouths lay down in the it
of you . . . You were home
from that time, and why
shouldn't you have been?

Imperialism failed. Such

startled years for the world.
Medium countries swelling,
little countries bleeding, big
countries turning into little countries
as they have since the start of time.
You stared out at the coast—
radio flowers of sound from Los Angeles,
boats dragging accidents
that hadn't happened . . . A gull flies
through two thirds of the shadow
of another gull . . .

You can't keep another person,
you know that. You had
to give them up—couldn't save them;
You lean left in the hut
and right in the magic. It's years
since you have missed them,
missed them most of all
while you were with them.
You broke free and spilled out
all the unreflected light they left
like the moon who has already
healed her nothing—

wasn't she triumphant
in her slim smile,
like one stripe peeled off a lighthouse;
they had added to your shadow
where you were,
you had become a little bit them
and were proud of the reflection,
proud of the crossing,
could expect to be recognized
where the day was undoing the day
and let the magic spread —-

L.A.—Berkeley   1969–1994

II

time

_____

alchemy

*As the universe cooled, radiation
and matter parted company.*

—John Boslough's commentary on
Stephen Hawking

*We apologize if your first choice of
entree is no longer available
by the time we reach your row.*

—American Airlines flight attendant,
Flight 496, June 1989

Cheap Gas

That dithyramb of ticky-tick, boom,
brrrrr we hear when we lift
the nozzle, pull back on the black rubber
and shove it in—

the noise hums to a bigger rumble,
practically shakes the self-serve pump;
probably it's the ancient forests
growing higher, reversing the Pleistocene—
they're refusing to become Techroline Super-Unleaded,
the trees have decided not to leave their bodies
in the rotting executive swamps.

Blackened thumbs hold the credit card slips
in the clipboard, the sweet young
men tear off "customer copy,"
look us in the eye. Their names in wilted
red letters over their hearts:
Jake, Carlos, Todd with two d's. We should
read the names carefully through fumes
rising from rainbows of spilled gas on the station floor,
still pretty cheap. Full tank 13.69.

Removing the nozzle we should notice,
when the vagrant drop falls down, the liquid is still
pretty golden, pink dominates for an instant,
then forgets.
Doesn't look like the blood of young men,
liquid from bodies: tears, semen, blood, urine,
acids, the yellow drop
of cheap gas has all those in it.   Bodies lie
in the sand and the ancient forests feel them over
and over and stop growing—

The Hanging Gardens of Nebuchadnezzar had one
of each kind of flower. We didn't bomb those.
The cruel king walked there with his personal servants;

we are his now.
We are tending the waters of cheap gas
where they fall. By the waters, slaves
lived for generations. By the waters
of Babylon they moved and spoke—

Male Nipples

—not utter, not
useless, the uselessness of desire, the slight
depression around the center

.

—When the motorcycle boy would light
        his cigarette, I longed
for the flat nipples, the scars, the contralto 'when'

.

and after you saw that the flower
of hell is not hell,
        but a flower—

.

How the beautiful boys' nipples in the pool
in Arizona looked
"underwatery"—pennies which have been thrown in

.

—and after you saw
that the flower of hell
was not one bit hell, but a flower—

.

convinced him to take only
his shirt off. They were, well, one
was brown and one was like the inside of a story—

.

—the ones of divers,
how they point down under the wetsuits:

.

        when I first put
my tongue on his (having decided
        he is not my mother)—

.

Oh, the bodies I loved were very tired.
I liked their skin. And
I was no sad animal no graveyard—

.

—and after you saw that desire
is hell, that the flower of hell
is not hell but a flower, well,

.

—So I told the little hairs
around his nipple: lie flat! and they did,
like a campfire, without the stories—

.

those of soldiers in the desert war and often
his left one tastes metallic as in
childhood, when I licked my brother's BB gun

.

Kept not finishing
        people I loved.
I tried, —but.

.

The top lip of a Corona beer
is about the size
of one of his—

.

      And after you saw that the flower
      of hell is desire, the almost, well,
you still had desire —

.

—So the moon came up
      pink tonight
like one of what had been missed

An Event

The worlds divided
and an event passed through time,
one that wasn't known

to cause the harm until it caused it . . .
(so, was the event
or was it *happening* the problem?)

The violence we know to be
the violence pushed it, the violence
underneath the violence pulled it

back through a sea-
mouth into the permanent
wild ocean that circulates the awe.

Chevron Tankers

if occasionally only several on the horizon one drags the absence
   of being

———————

when halfway across the window the jagged one has stopped
   this nervousness that won't continue

———————

where is "below" in them or is the oil confined such that it won't
   continue

———————

the ensign comes up from the boiler room; I'd like to see the
   Admiral, I say

———————

Chevron dragging the shattered opals across the bay; they don't
   intend to but not intending is the brutality that could
   enfold you

———————

some of the tankers seem to have guns on your birthday

———————

the ensign comes up from the boiler room; I'm sorry he says
   the Admiral can't see you

———————

parts of it made no sense but neither did Chevron

———————

absence of being with hooks on its forehead

———————

oil slopping underneath in sections as reality must have sections
        which could damage birds

———————

and vats of weak color you could look down into

———————

the ensign comes up from the boiler room; I'm sorry, the Admiral
        misinformed you

———————

what would you want to eat after they had sailed reasonably
        over the pink starfish who gossip

———————

if you use it fear it

———————

oil which once was opal beauty under the ice with a war which
        got into the wings of birds

———————

past sailboats to the hooks on their foreheads the d's and f's
        on their foreheads

———————

if you use it

34

(visitor fragments)

Had been doing meditations on depression and alchemy
after the Gulf "conflict," trying to recall mercury and feminine
nature, had discerned a figure with the eyes of an owl or a
walnut half who could come and go inside a circle and with-
draw; had thought she had more power but it turned out she
was simply less likely to be visible.

Having thought of her as a kind of muse
who would bring sustenance
I could not then

Having thought of her as a kind of (   )
who shone in a circle
when I asked I could not then

(—Having thought of her
as a kind of direction, who,
when I asked I could not then—)

Not a figure who was sent.to help
but as some "one" to talk into, who
would be stately under these conditions,
who would not dance.

Trying, I

The visitor coming—

(I was trying to chronicle her exits:

the visitor coming
in and out of the ring my very tiredness
had created for her;

and I understood she had no control
over the units
and, of course, I didn't either—)

I looked up from my reading;

the mind is a limitless universe.

Something that looked like her teeth
on the bedside table;

where was she anyway
who came when I asked her
but left at her own pleasure?

my you?

my her?

(not minding that she appeared with holes
for eyes, the uncontrollable being shaped

by cold time, into a miracle)

visitor
my visitor come back
into the cave   I can't stand

    the days when you are gone

Proud Energy

After the wildfires our cities are brighter
at sunset. Doctors with carphones
and the young leave work early to watch
the dragon streaks of orange. In the hills,
new energy as the rattlesnakes plan
stamina among the dry coyote bushes;
coastal winds with warm
and all-mothering powers blow
ashes of brush fires up from LA
over the homeless on the avenues, a backless
song of the conquered and the conqueror,
since California is its own muse . . .

In town, people we've stepped over all day
rise to get dinner in the churches.
Mostly pasta on doubled paper plates.
They put boiled eggs in their pockets
for later, as Saturn's shadow might
swallow its small moons. When is the moment
the prophets arrive? Curled carrots
look lively and pierced. The addicts eat fast,
but others put extra bread slowly in bags,
bread with proud energy passed from the sun
to the wheat will help the people back
to the avenue, to unlearn the directions,

they stagger toward standing—
(can you remember standing as a baby
before you learned your boundaries too well?)
Sunset on the leather faces, asking for money;
should we give it to them (you survivor—)
and whom do we work for? the family?
for the guy with tassels on his loafers
or for the coiled internal snake
that's happy only after we've fed it
the small mammal of the unexpected?

Beside us, the goodbye-love generation
awaits the prophetic moment—

And if there's no prophetic moment?
No lightning instructions from the root
of the laurel, no fire congress
at the center of the world, if we can't even say
Not this time clearly into them, maybe
if we just notice one thing: look
at the buttons for instance: how many are there?
Look at the corner of the eyes: moisture
triangles, sleep scum . . . We wanted the perfect
heart but the energy didn't spin
one of those. The imperfect heart
of love is not looking away—

No Problem

The expression No problem began to be used around the time silk
        plants became more realistic, even being made with silk
        aphids and silk diseases.

Only a few shopkeepers used No problem in 1985. The man
        in the aquarium store uprooted violet algae with a small
        spade.

When pieces of the Wall began to be sold, there was a lot of No
        problem but it was mostly a food service expression.

By the time Romania hit the delivery people used it and
        the Nooooh had a waterslide in it; problem was quicker.

After Bush offered Mrs. Chamorro 100 million and surprise surprise
she took it, he might have said it to mean you're welcome.

When they started selling uniforms of dead Iraqi soldiers, people in
        doorways whose eaten-out tennis shoes lined up with their
        dogs' Styrofoam cups used it and so did poets.

Somewhat Anthem

Address to the triple figure deprived

of sunsets right now

in election time whom do we elect

squares of simple shadows coming down

who would help others help them

we scratched the scraps for the nonevent

put our heads on the table to ask again

the table a rusted prairie all aflame

ivy climbed that building that latin of leaves

crickets in books a muffled excellence

———————————

A man lay in front of the library on an arm

air a glazed pavilion surrounding him

light struck the error of his right face

lemon savage mercury

lifting was calmer than the second time

we offered him food that was stranger of us

a version of what we were already thinking

at the end of this the poorest space of time

only some deep noticing was possible

and some spare change

_____

Filling out the ballot it's hard to aim

inevitably overfilling the squares

we were the citizens of the missing flame

what if at the end of personal healing

this is why I've called you up dear one

Paracelsus not having succeeded

what with chlorine in the water

this is being written on ancient scraps I–XII

filling out the ballots during the metal

table squeaking of the polling volunteers

_____

I saw the four of swords reversed

the ten of pentacles people twirling stars in wheels

wise economy in conflict with yawn and riches

and I was aware of you hovering in the trees

your fragrant moon your metalwork your healing

what could we do but spend less money

the prone one lying on his arm

others using lattés for transformation

chocolate into foam into coffee into

and on the side streets

those cakes still dreaming of vanilla

_____

And we were aware of you hovering

in the trees not counting the ballots our

little fear surveys

Grenada various gulfs Somalia Haiti

a prone one lying on her arm

Creusa having stumbled from the ruins

and if at the end of personal healing

no one helped was helped what then

for those who could never what then

love was between us and the time of them

_____

And we were aware of you hovering

lifted our heads from the ballots

the gray planks handed to the polling volunteers

and if at the close of the personal what then

voting even if hurt

not like the flag like the wind

each controlled by a different what then

fragrant moon metalwork

the alchemy of trying again

water working the deepest fields

index   universe   other

III

alchemy

_____

problem

The heart hid still in the dark,
hard as a philosopher's stone.

—Paul Celan, *Collected Prose*
(Waldrop translation)

The Bat

Something had been started—   a sound
not profoundly "won over"   —   we were cooking

trying to use less noise;

it seemed not
to want anything to be changed to be done—   caught in
      a light fixture

(the beginning needed an opening)

Lucifer, nasty, then
      very resentful

A false sense of light
having been sent—the bat caught in the light fixture

Something had just been said about an invitation
      ("tell him not to do it")

The habit of asking
the universe what it needs

      Once released onto the carpet—onto the subject:
oh the flat, the mistake mouse

It had been caught
under plastic as eternity is caught, in time

      through an open window
to the trees then. It was not a concern,—

The problem of what
to do next, how to feel, foregone . . .

Briefly, the beyond comes to us—

Symmetry Breaking

Poking at the airplane meal. Lots of the same Utah over the—
      not sure what to call it—   chicken with
      the flap of itself on top.

At the beginning of time, matter decided to form clumps to stop
      the symmetry. *(Decided* is what I believe.) Small groundhog-
      looking dinner roll. Was the Dairy Blend conceived in the
      original flame? The aluminum came off so easily.

One distended lettuce leaf loose as the unconsciousness of
      the classics we bring along. Travelers are always so hungry.
      Plutarch writes of the soldiers in the Parthian campaign
      they fight till they're starving and fall on the poison herbs.

After a split second the universe said goodbye to evenness.
      What must it have been thinking. Matter began. Why?
      It must have been so odd before. The event had been
      safely resisted . . .

And now this triangle of Cool Whip with its more than successful
      chocolate sprinkles.

It's hardly apparent who will travel. The ninth grade diagram of cell
      division. Some stay to the left; some, having been kissed
      get onto the plane.

	texture
	shape
would you like the	missing
Chicken Kiev or the	mouth
Lasagna	wanderer

C ode

when it moves up the alder
only its red C moves

          the- the- the-
    feels sorry for it

    the red-headed woodpecker
in front of *ofness,* moved before the tree

As envy feels sorry
    for the thing envied, after

C for career of searching, for the solid thing

    As for the red on his head: the hydrant stuck in snow
    feels "sorry" for it

A sharp cry from the schoolboy in the snow
    pierced the slipping C!

    And texture took the position the bird
    moved against

(The dim cry of my love
    in his fever)

The bird moved against, a universe unscaled

Patches of striving

(Where my love in his fever   lay down)

River Song

Panic diagonals
their river-method duck's-head breath

You preferred the park
 before the leaves came out

Later was too late for the river fronds
to unbraid the hair of the raven

The moon has two birthdays
you're the personal servant of taillights

Spectator of day's finest closing

At dusk you apologize

The colors forgive you because they change

. . . and said the poem
would show me the way.

—What way, I asked.

—The ways.

blue codices

(a cycle of poems on
depression and alchemy)

*Explain the unknown by
the more unknown.*

—an alchemical theorem

the cliffs

For a while, the great secret
wasn't apparent to you: what you thought
you should become, you wouldn't . . .

You faced the blue (the favored?) direction
and hoped for something beyond 'the permanent'—

So: this sorrow you're experiencing again; you don't
have to "work on it";

if they show you a candle uncovered
in the sea cave can't you just
approach it like an ocean

from which nothing was selected
            but everything had been kept—

—Let's just, by mixing rain   "how to start   first stage—
   on the Golden Gate   without starting"
with sulfur force   mercury—
                                                     two snakes—

                                        wrapped in the nameless again

doubting chamber

I went to the doubting chamber
thinking there would be a change.

Where could the new words
come from. Speak to me, ravens.
(The ravens didn't answer.)

I asked the law,
which is the dream,
becoming wilder
without differences

and I saw there were so many
in my heart I figured only one of us
had to change, for there to be a change—

<table>
<tr><td></td><td></td><td>agency</td></tr>
<tr><td>second stage:</td><td>they lied about</td><td>viceroy</td></tr>
<tr><td>he set his flask on the fire</td><td>the root canal;</td><td></td></tr>
<tr><td></td><td>the pink ^ equals</td><td>"and probably you just</td></tr>
<tr><td></td><td>two weeks</td><td>about were"</td></tr>
</table>

horizontal series

(Come in, you said
but the day did not hear you.
And you saw for the first time

it wouldn't be as you supposed,
the heart would always hurt
from not being chosen;

doves lined the longing streets
with their east-colored silks, their latitudes—
you didn't have to be just like those,

you could pretend the other magic
also had returned,
even if it hadn't)

his depression, his   third stage—sublimation
  writing it's hopeless, he'll   Jupiter: dry refinement and I explained the rules
try the new drug   of football to her:
                                            "wide receiver"

deep noticing

There was a deep noticing
around the tent;

they say, for a transformation
to be made you'd have to
give up the gravity
of a broken self but that's ridiculous;

if the mystery doesn't want to be known
it sees you from the secret ground

as those seeds with
spiked tongues (or wings?) traveling
through the woods will be opened
only in the great fires—

                                fourth stage:
little boys' finished funeral
   mixing with   —cough syrup stain
"but left the library   (they never   around the mouth
   dizzy with hope"   took your side)   of the moon—

trap door

You fell into the stretchy gold trap
of the promise,
a life that draws its instinct from the general
glow of what has been expected of it: down

the self goes with the dragon: fixed
achievement!   wingless & bare—   What's

something is so unusual as you pass it!
hovering as it does over the ledge
of every moment's hope

and you are killed
while you are nothing, though consciousness is
supposed to be the welcome of it, and the door . . .

fifth stage   [I'm sorry it's difficult;
                               she put the card   any easier
                               into the ATM—punched—,   would be a lie]
Venus did not visit   no sunlight

"oh sir   we are defeated"

spiral lullaby

The agony
that lives nowhere
but in a choice;

each action makes the next one
more unbearable . . .

You came from plain life as the black squirrel
comes from two trees to the right
            and with this practice you'll

return to it,—ting, ting, new

            night bird (the spiral ting
of old dropped silverware);   sleep now, as you die

            to the old self

                    not best   but only—

sixth stage: a veritable
the chemical wedding, not   Well, I just
        sorrow of mind   got tired of letting them   stonehenge of candles
                                        came up and it seemed
                                        like they were useless

below below

In the corner of the heart
reserved for action, a pig is eating
the poppies of hell;

it doesn't look up when I come in;
it doesn't need
a confirming ideal. If there are flowers

there must be dirt below hell
where power has no meaning
but growth comes out of it.

Now a door blows open
and this sound starts coming in
till enough of the candles are lit—

stage 7—the thought
of sorrow not as an event   the alchemist grew hopeful
                            as the vapor rose

red-breasted nuthatch—
    hello you wonderful!

    (then, the federal
    deficit . . .)

the escalator

Is there in each act
a little pocket of magic?
When you rode with your mother

in a minor city, looking down, you saw
the differences: additional rain from the umbrella
dripped into the rain-looking steps of the escalator—

then: 2 rains,—then, 3!   wove together.
Holiday cheer—something pulled the sides
of people's cheeks until they smiled . . .

but once in the air again, you felt
the spaces form inside
to free you from pleasure's oppression—

working on the ";"
she kept on laughing

burned fields
during elections (contrasting with
    new warblers:
mouth 'bands'—or smudges?)

the cave

(I have a garden that grows in the dark
but I never found you,
unknown beauty

so what good is this work? feeling along
the sides of the cave, often going
outside where flowers just as dear have chosen
the supplemental glamour of reality . . .

And if at the end of healing there is nothing?

I try to rejoice but I was placed
between worlds to hear
what you so easily gave up, unknown beauty—)

as the red appeared   (fortunately her popsicle
they swore the bird flew   —and I was aware of you   set down
from the athanor, that   hovering in the trees—   by the phone had left
    pan of ashes   a red 'pitchfork'

visitor fragment

Lately the visitor
looks the same as the enemy; why
should I agree to see her?

She withdraws to the various
outposts I invented earlier . . .

My visitor is on the other side,
I can't see her from
the ring of fire I've been assigned;

what am I to her now
since I am what I was when
the mild thing I said
had not delighted her—

a depression not characterized   silver confetti

(but my hand heard when
the instructions started
to panic)

by "advance"—not coming

out of it

various outposts

You traded places
with the mystery—fire-torn, insulated leaves,
the steady eyes of the huckleberry—   (Haven't you

been sad most of your life? Come on,
all those outposts in the middle . . . then they say the end
of growth is that you'll suffer "purely" . . .)

One night, remember? No envy or hope.
What you sought
was here, what was done

could not be undone by you: there was the owl,
the night's vice president,
the tangled sheets of moon—

their faces
   like killed paint—   —salamanders   tenth stage:
                          —sylphs   the fire had to cling
                          —undines   to what it ate—
                          —gnomes

high vortex

At some time you will come to know
how even an event you "mastered" wasn't yours
because you were conduit for family sorrow

(you triangle, space the salty spirits rented);

isn't there a whirl
inside experience that helps unlive it?—maybe—

When you stood on the cliff, when
a little loudness rushed from the earth
and shook, no one said to it cheer up Quartz! (because
of what it had seen—)   Of course

it tilted coming from down there. As one's too-brightly
hurrying out a gate is unequal, but being—

stage II
 no guilt   (in the air—
          unfinished,
 the squirrel holding its paw   manageable—
  like Napoleon

          it will stop—)

blue square

When I gave up hope of being complete,
the sorrow deepened.
As that went too, a mystery replaced it.

Now it's a faint blue square against which being
and nonbeing will always
wrestle, even in the afterlife . . .

Spiders move raindrops over flat
woolly webs as stars wheel through Andromeda Galaxy.
Light that left those stars when humans

first stood up is just now getting here . . .
Beyond that, the alchemists remake the worlds
from what rises and falls, vapor and distillate—

twelfth stage—   she had gotten to   (I know what I want to
                            "dangling participles"

was it a failure   say to them . . .)

IV

problem

_____

time

The Captain: *Can you make the past
go faster?*

The Guardian: *I was made to offer the
past in this manner; I cannot change.*

The Captain: *Spock and I will go back
into time itself and attempt to
change it.*

—*Star Trek*

*So it is meaningless to ask which is
real, "real" or "imaginary" time;
it is simple a matter of which is
the most useful description.*

—Stephen Hawking

Time's Body

—in the middle of the beginning they woke you
from a long sleep;

you could see the edges of the world
being formed, the boundaries
space would make in its eagerness
to be included,

the problem time would have
in its need to be the main thing.

The source of life is not life
but rebellion toward meaning.

When you saw the workers were already busy,
that the list you'd been handed
was usual and impossible
and held it all, and thin
or most, your will
strong as a paper clip

you needed a location
from which to act on your assigned nature

so you chose time:
seed of light,
seed of torment—

All right, you didn't
have to do it
all at once—

Time Problem

The problem
of time.   Of there not being
enough of it.

My girl came to the study
and said Help me;
I told her I had a time problem
which meant:
I would die for you but I don't have ten minutes.
Numbers hung in the math book
like motel coathangers.   The Lean
Cuisine was burning
like an ancient city: black at the edges,
bubbly earth tones in the center.
The latest thing they're saying is lack
of time might be
a "woman's problem." She sat there
with her math book sobbing—
(turned out to be prime factoring: whole numbers
dangle in little nooses)
Hawking says if you back up far enough
it's not even
an issue, time falls away into
'the curve' which is finite,
boundaryless. Appointment book,
soprano telephone—
(beep End beep went the microwave)

The hands fell off my watch in the night.
I spoke to the spirit
who took them, told her: Time is the funniest thing
they invented. Had wakened from a big
dream of love in a boat—
No time to get the watch fixed so the blank face
lived for months in my dresser,
no arrows

for hands, just quartz intentions, just the pinocchio
nose   (before the lie)
left in the center;   the watch
didn't have twenty minutes; neither did I.

My girl was doing
her gym clothes by herself;   (red leaked
toward black, then into the white
insignia)   I was grading papers,
heard her call from the laundry room:
Mama?
Hawking says there are two
types of it,
real and imaginary   (imaginary time must be
like decaf), says it's meaningless
to decide which is which
but I say: there was tomorrow-
and-a-half
when I started thinking about it; now
there's less than a day. More
done. That's
the thing that keeps being said. I thought
I could get more done as in:
fish stew from a book. As in: Versateller
archon, then push-push-push
the tired-tired around the track like a planet.
Legs, remember him?
Our love—when we stagger—lies down inside us . . .
Hawking says
there are little folds in time
(actually he calls them wormholes)
but I say:
there's a universe beyond
where they're hammering the brass cut-outs . . .
Push us out in the boat and leave time here—

(because: where in the plan was it written,
You'll be too busy to close parentheses,
the snapdragon's bunchy mouth needs water,
even the caterpillar will hurry past you?

Pulled the travel alarm
to my face: the black
behind the phosphorous argument kept the dark
from being ruined. Opened
the art book
—saw the languorous wrists of the lady
in Tissot's "Summer Evening." Relaxed. Turning
gently. The glove
(just slightly—but still:)
"aghast";
opened Hawking, he says, time gets smoothed
into a fourth dimension
but I say
space thought it up, as in: Let's make
a baby space, and then
it missed. Were seconds born early, and why
didn't things unhappen also, such as
the tree became Daphne . . .

At the beginning of harvest, we felt
the seven directions.
Time did not visit us. We slept
till noon.
With one voice I called him, with one voice
I let him sleep, remembering
summer years ago,
I had come to visit him in the house of last straws
and when he returned
above the garden of pears, he said
our weeping caused the dew . . .

I have borrowed the little boat
and I say to him Come into the little boat,
you were happy there;

the evening reverses itself, we'll push out
onto the pond,
or onto the reflection of the pond,
whichever one is eternal—

Band Practice

—I dropped her off, she was balancing the guitar case
on her head, there was one of those abnormal green
ladybugs on the front seat; I said:
call me anyway even if you're happy—

Busy Week

Being Busy

—Dots of blue permission
came out of your head;
you were thinking faster, and the part
that couldn't think said, Don't despair;

but you had to be quiet
in relation to the cave, to study sentences,
because you'd never learned
not to be busy, they
had helped you to be busy,
you worked harder until,

of the three
kinds of logic, you had learned four—

Very Busy

—Everyone talked about how much
busier they were. Friends
became the type
that could work on a poem while driving . . .

Malls with fountains did too much
(you didn't have to go along with that)
but slowing down took time too (Something
missing here?)   Or

maybe you could read less. The novels
wouldn't mind. Snails made little Niles with their bodies
till flatness is what they saw,

moved with silk instinct
when they moved from doubt
though not
getting it done was the accomplishment—

Really Busy

—You yelled at the broken sunbeam
Slow down!
(It hurried across the office, having passed

an event that hadn't happened . . .)
What's to be done about busyness?
but how could the sunbeam help.

An island learned the water's face
because the water had surrounded it . . .
If you can't do less

you can count and
if you can't calm down at least
tell them you're not coming—

—Days of not
seeing her then seeing her then
thinking I had
seen her and not seeing her—

The Particles

"Various combinations of these twelve particles are
thought to make up everything in the material world."

New York Times science page

A.   The leptons

    tau

        her hair

    electron

        her rushing

    muon

        herself, rushing

    neutrino

        Her brown—

    neutrino

        her little

    neutrino

        hr

B.   The quarks

    up

        her dawn leaping

down

        her curry

charm

        made tea

strange

        her poem

bottom

        her bath

top

        is

Time Zone

—I hate being out of your time zone.
It hurts like being matter
when light got called away, at first,

and the clock inside the warbler's breast
started up, the yellow shirt you wore when we
first kissed got its heartbeat pressed so far in the cloth

the night came out the back;
first we were darkness, then we were galaxies,
traveling too fast too far for me to call

throughout all that space goodbye
my twin my half
of the light, goodbye my little bit famous—

Early Vacations

Morning in the mountains: a greenish warbler hops between
      bushes after it's been identified. He has taken the girls
      to ride the twisted cable on the slope through what he keeps
      referring to as "light pouring down." Today, it does not
      descend, it rises.
A man walks along exactly at eye level,
the complicated stones giving him only half of each step.
Then this dizziness adding to it. The children come back
      with bruised flowers. Yellow-white-lavender
                           behind the fence of Z's.
Imperfect horses before happiness sets in,
a happiness almost too much to bear.

*

Their black caps
pulled tight over their heads, the jays watch us
like the executioners of Robespierre.
Apostrophes of dead twigs hang down on four sides in seven
      dimensions: right left, front back, up down, time.
Windowboxes of blood geraniums. Maybeck windows:
diamonds of glass.

*

In the shades of changing, swimming out to the boulders
      he looked so beautiful. The girls made intricate
      sand fortresses near the adolescents who enjoyed
      the distress of their bodies.
How to surprise him. I have no gift for surprise. The water
      is intolerable. How can he? Made of a dead volcano, the
      lake's magic holds the need to change, the tongue of fire
      on the lips of water.
The rescue boat scuds out. The farther I swim the wider the gap
      between us. Finally I reach him and we swim side by side
      to the padded steel raft.

*

The voices of the girls from behind the house make the stumps
        dance, all just the same. He types, sometimes reversing
        what he does, so the machine bleats like a dump truck.
Here's how the wave on the lake looks (there is just one wave):
        like a small laugh.
        A strip of white then a strip of tan then a strip of white
        that can't decide. It said: I'll let you see behind me. It said:
        What green and-blue?
        The green that is far from the ocean. The blue
        an approach, not making fun of us.

*

Bundles of delicious
fat on the woman tanning; then she goes into the lake.
Our magazine spread out: Khomeini's fanatics, hundreds of
        faces over caskets so collapsed they've forgotten their dead.
Reagan, his nose gashed from surgery, his hanging jowl, the new
        failed peace plan, and set between columns of print,
        a Contra—belts of long bullets like the pegs for
        some vacation game.

*

Then he swam far out to the buoy.
I couldn't see his head but the girls said they saw it.
I didn't want to look so hard on the horizon. (Several jays
approach the deck now; the water I looked for him in
was the color of the jay as it flies selfishly off.)
What I notice about thinking is, a cylinder of creation happens
        after the first thought.
The first thought was, God took my joy.
The second thought was no.

*

He comes onto the deck below with one shoe untied,
his face lined with the expression I now recognize as The Past.
After standing there a while he resumes his typing: muffled
        iambs, a pillow placed over the heart.

*

The girls shoulder their butterfly nets on the trail.
Earlier they practiced the sweep.
Not so much watching as joining, just for a second to be that
        fluttering inside the net, not so much the thing as
        frightened light, not so much the light as the verb before
it turns nounlike, the moment before, before it
corresponds to being "caught."

*

The crayfish we caught crowded the sides of the big pan.
The girls held them up for me to see. Their backs a sisterly pink and
orange, a withheld sunset under blue shells. Everything
lovely has attributes of permanent longing. Time fate irony light:
the crayfish clawed their way through that list. We lay on the pier
and hung over the edge. He caught fifteen, the girls caught
ten, I caught two. I would have caught more but I saw this bloated
figure of a muse in the water. He knew just how
to lower the line among the huge boulders.
One crayfish would come out like a poem, the most obvious part
first and grab the custardy chicken fat and pull it;
I'd try to reel it up and he would put the net
                           under the crayfish
who was straining to hold on, life's avarice holding on to non-
life's infinity. He said the creature did not "feel" anything.
I admired that.
But the blue-and-amber backs had matched the world they lived in
        for one terrifying moment. And the violent orange
        they changed to was beautiful only because we'd memorized
        the other color, knew what they had been.

V

time

_____

space

The Unbeginning

—or, maybe you could just
give up on beginnings. After all,

this notion that things start
and end somewhere
has caused you so much trouble!

Look at the wild radish in the fields out there.
Isn't it always row
and row of pastel pink-
yellow-blue like some bargain
print of itself, in new pillowcases, on sale;

and you stumble
through it thinking art must come
from the book of splendor
or the book of longing
until the rhythms curve

and the previous music
hasn't ended yet:

the whir the blackbirds make,
as they land, sound like velcro,
like a child undoing
velcro from the winter jacket

(from the *hood*
of a winter jacket)

The Mysteries

Writing about the mysteries
you can't quite say what they were.
Sacrifices? fasting? walking below
or sprinkling drops of water near
the marriage bed where the celebrants lay
briefly with the sacred one before
the raising up of objects?
You, the writer separated from her
by centuries, know only that later she'll
reappear sometimes on vases . . .
Hell was invented about this time;
later sources aren't reliable.

Aristotle writes that you'll suffer
over the mysteries but will learn
nothing new. The past slips into you finally.
Generations kept these secrets.
Islands fell asleep looking at the sea.
The one who ruled you above will rule you
below, taking you down to show you
the cut part of the wheat.
Probably she was earth,
your hunger was beautiful,
her hunger was beautiful,
but what do you really know?

Much was enacted, much was shown,
the burning one is sought
as an emblem; just once you will lie down
between her legs. The ritual
goes on with its potions,
its implied promises; the priest goes on
with his combs, his animals,
the exhausted wheat held up—
you try in vain, and after your research
among the transcripts of the institution

what gives you immortal life turns out to be
the breath of another person . . .

Belief in the subterranean rooms
has haunted you. Not finding them
isn't it the same as if you had?
We know you through your writings
and your complaints. Of course
she found you, though you believed
she loved you less than she should have—
your short smile, your long tears,
your fingers exiting the page,
the chords of your mysteries
absolute and wild and brief—

LOOSE SUGAR

(12 pieces from behind the slides)

. . . and indeed, when invoking the name and
destiny of women, one thinks more of the space
generating and forming the human species than
of *time* . . .

> —Julia Kristeva,
> "Women's Time"

Today Brazil is an industrialized underdeveloped
country marked by contradiction and uncertainty.

> —Luis Bresser Pereira,
> *Development and Crisis in Brazil*

(The need to understand
how children listen. To do that
before going on . . .)

Two Rivers

The spirits are raining. This is true because of airplane breath.

A "day" slips back and forth in time.

I make numbers, my mother's darkness to the left, soon she'll be
      the curve in a 5.

A secret can be used in public if not done in a row. Fix your face
      so they know you are listening, then think your new word.
      Today's new word is stewardess.

In the now of this she points from the airplane: the lines of Brazil
      are simply there

where the dark & lighter rivers join, the joining is

a tiny slash (/).

For a time I dissolved upon my mother's tongue . . .

Rio Preto, she says. Amazon from the right (girl / boy, dark / light
      which should I prefer)

Both rivers have fish that could eat a girl in minutes.

It's not that I can't choose between them but why bother—

If I'm made to decide . . .

(which is why I begin to love metaphor)

"and dwelt for a while in a foreign land"

National Development

What is development?

Our father's job is to "aid development."
>   He stands in the sugar fields at a fazenda being outlined
>   next to shiny stalks with one stalk in his hands. When he
>   smiles, the world succeeds.

Brazil is my mother's country; it is second.

During the *then* of this, President Vargas has died in a square of
>   circumstance. During the now we are developed.

Secret time spirits—(Can many hide if only some succeed?)

In the apartment, our mother's body is the loved interval
>   that leaks out loving and sometimes goes out twice;

we are among the middle classes, which means we have a servant.

Running—   in a blur, toward being better—

while I was there
held captive

I disagreed with the concept of "line"—

(sometimes the text looks down like an adult
when you're trying to remember the content—)

Two Mothers

We had two mothers who shifted their same borders like
       countries. One did our best;

the other put secret sugar in our milk; stirred it; laughed.

Bosses of sweetness built Brasilia out of little nerves.

How to live without the concept of "being better"?

In the door to the left I start to feature her as the space;

I love her more than I am not here;
she loves us more though near is never reached.

Less fond of eating, I practice numbers;

the moment curve meets straight in the 5 is the "point" where
       time meets space.

At the moment it is missing I start to love her—;   (or,

at the moment I start to fear it I start to love her)

(notes from other people's books)

inflation 26% in 1954
what happened to President Vargas?
when Kubitschek came to power he believed in Brazil
middle classes growing—not strange to find modern
machines in family factories.
the idea of the fifties can be seen in the figure below.
fazenda owners wanted no industry but K realized no econ.
        develop. w/o foreign inv.
no denying foreign

Sugar Chart
(in millions of tons)

	1950	1957	1958	1959
Brazil	1401	2714	3004	3108

(the voice can stop horizontally)

Two Brothers

I have doubted my belief in sentences because of their
        refusal to recall certain things.

A way of being satisfied. A sound.

So the wish to restore them "arose"—

Walking with two brothers down Copacabana in the fifties
        city of gold teeth *açucar* such nerves,

a developing time sandwich holding hands on the black and
        white sidewalk, wavy like the graph of a patient who
        has not been born yet,—

our six feet shuffling through childhood my brothers' sea babble
        delicious remedy keeping me mixed with them;

Love comes from nothing but it comes.

Maybe it's not that day but near it; a loose agitated brightness
        that needs rescuing . . .

The spirits will work anywhere: past the vanilla courtyards'
        foam, sound flies, shells of grub cravings;

each word makes an outline come out of a body.

"To think" means: the looseness is taken away.

(having doubts about events
because events aren't deep enough)

Stuck Tram

In childhood, time was a particle game when it
      was in a row.

Down or up is certainly a problem when something is stuck.

A tram car stalled toward Sugar Loaf in 1956.

She and I later disagree on the length of the stall, which proves
      we aren't each other.

And the spirit world burned sweetly , yonder . . .

An Olympic runner in the tram with us—our *brush with fame* —

A memory,

followed by (—in a dendrite, with a synapse fixed by neuroreceptors,

something casually developed, like a dirt road in a developing
      country)

the alleged self

composed of time dots: not remembering whether we
never got to the mountain

or just had trouble
getting there—

(tired of senators saying we must
        "triumph over darkness")

———————————

Loose Sugar

I hardly remember any sounds from childhood.
Leaving them out is second . . .

Little boys from the favelas came to the apartment for sugar.

In the smooth language I will later lose she gives it to them:

tin cupfuls to their twin existences.

        (How blind the sugar is, being passed along
and tumbling into little bodies

helplessly)

Everyone would have sacrificed something for them not
        to have to ask for it.

All our fathers stood in cane fields in some respect.

Later—the rest of my life—time resembles warm sugar,
        something almost imaginary having to do with asking.

In what part of early to hide the particular?

Those boys are dead now; in the street perhaps their children's
        children are roving bands of thieves . . .

When I was a child
in a blur   toward being better
I disagreed with the concept of "need"—

(time as short stanzas that went on
replacing each other)

Red Fingernails

Briefly I dwelt upon my mother's tongue . . .

They put up a swingset in the lobby where we liked to hang.
        Red fingernails. The polish had been an intoxicant.

Rubber trees spoke with red lips. Talking with the spirits then
        didn't seem all that necessary.

President Kubitschek is doing his best to welcome the post-
        colonial companies.

My mother rejoins her first language so she can live, and in
        making numbers, I developed a love of the partially hollow;

the other mother tried to give us her body, painting our fingernails
        in the kitchen, it was like growing sunsets.

During this time we rarely spoke English; we understood
        because of what they didn't say.

What happened is not how we should measure things.

Joy exists because there are delays:

those intervals in bodies where two languages mix

before the first one has to be lifted away—

(being truthful made the surface
sort of grainy—)

Vanilla Continued

A mother's sentence wrenched from her body makes
  the unfillable interval.

. . . Running through the recent word to get to the ice cream
  truck—*sorvete!*

Now we know time as an exchange of energy. How did it feel
  to have to change languages when my mother went north
  to marry.

The awning is stretched over the smeared day—sugar's sister,
  vanilla, we run to the corner streets of Rio

inside her word for it.

A mother equals how little we have of her plus

the fullness her language signifies
  (to use the word some people like).

What the child sees does not see back.
  It's where metaphor comes from . . .

To make a happiness on sidewalks you can walk across
  spirit particles between the little cracked nerves—

(talking with friends about whether
            "art" "mirrors" "nature")

The Corcovado

These lines settle like the flakes of some mineral.

One stone god hangs above Rio to forgive it;

we assumed we'd get wiser when confronted with him.

I put my face on his alleged leg while visitors looked at the view
            and I heard the crystals move.

Being a citizen is like being one of his mosaic pieces, your parents
            can't always help while the ruins assemble you;

I stood there while the non-suicide leaders developed the fifties
            falling in love with the boy god because the particles
            of quartz were trapped in him, the lyric moment
            a trillion times of being helped by specific sand in his
            blind stone robe.

Intuition tells you to store things as your salvation. When
            there's no mirror, the dark becomes loved.

(was it "post-colonial"?)

Beach Photos

I'm interested in the strip of mineral light around family slides
       of everybody on the same towel.

(We are given families we sometimes don't recognize.

They stay as "subject matter" stays with us even after we have
       punched a hole in *about.)*

On the southern beaches of Brazil my brothers hunted little frogs—
       sapinhos—in the blind spots of time . . .

They (we) were glad; families later disagree on who was glad.

Development nearly flattens the fifties. Time is warm and sweet.
       Our mother's body attracts most attention on the beach with
       her white and strawberry suit;

I who have feared outline swell to contain her, write *about* her
       though   *about*   has a hole in it . . .

What does it mean for a country to be "on its feet"?

Possibly the sand washed down from Sugar Loaf Mountain and lay
       at our feet . . .

When I see the grainy surface of a screen before the slides are shown

I have the urge to eat it—

(the lyric you worked really hard to retrieve)

Mother's Language

Maybe you dwelt for a brief time in a language given up for you

or found reasons to combine brightnesses like a picture of a
       Brazilian village made of butterfly wings—;

why are children still thought of as incomplete?

Your fingers were so smooth
       because your fingerprints had been stolen!

To this very day,
before or after a photo, thinking sentences will heal you,

you stand so straight your speech is slow.

You speak to her so well now!

And if what she thinks she gave up is not what she
       gave up, there is a desperate sweetness—

(without mirrors)

Remembering Form

Early life was a looseness;

even if your preferred mode is fragment, you need syntax
    to love.

Still, there is a "leaking" when we try to put things together.

As a bowl starts out being a bowl, the not-bowlness
    drains out of it. Later,

form is not something we remember doing, like being born.

We are lived by what we didn't have, which is not the same as
    saying we distinguish it,

though sometimes the outline of my husband's ear in the half dark
    looks like Brazil—

world/axis

That she would come to meet you
as if to solve the enigma of your being . . .

The feminine might bend the light—

   (It could involve seeming
   recognized or sought—)

The visitor comes,
not an invention but
an axis of something already invented—

(even memory is sometimes an invention
   as are dreams)

—her left arm curved like a galaxy.

Others sang disarmingly among the stars.

NOTE

p. 58   On the form of *blue codices:* Below the furnace, the ash.

ACKNOWLEDGMENTS

Many thanks to the editors and staff of the following magazines for publishing these poems: *Agni Review, American Poetry Review, Antaeus, Bellingham Review, Berkeley Poetry Review, Boston Review, Colorado Review, Electronic Poetry Review, 14 Hills* (*The SFSU Review*), *Harvard Review, The Iowa Review, Marlboro Review, Michigan Quarterly Review, The New Yorker, New American Writing, Pharos* (Paris), *Poetry U.S.A., ROOMS, 6ix, Slate,* and *VOLT.*

"The Spark" was reprinted in *Each Poem Alive* (Norton), and "Male Nipples" was reprinted in *The Male Body* (University of Michigan Press).

I am also very grateful to the Guggenheim Foundation for a fellowship which helped me to complete this book.

Thanks also to Joshua Clover, Dale Going, Robert Hass, Laura Mullen, Leslie Scalapino, Carol Snow, and 'Annah Sobelman for reading the work in this manuscript in advance of publication.

"Loose Sugar" is for HFH.

UNIVERSITY PRESS OF NEW ENGLAND publishes books under its own imprint and is the publisher for Brandeis University Press, Dartmouth College, Middlebury College Press, University of New Hampshire, Tufts University, and Wesleyan University Press.

ABOUT THE AUTHOR

Brenda Hillman is the author of *Coffee, 3 A.M.* (1982) and four other books of poetry published by Wesleyan University Press, *White Dress* (1985), *Fortress* (1989), *Death Tractates* (1992), and *Bright Existence* (1993). Her work has won the Delmore Schwartz Memorial Award for Poetry and the Poetry Society of America's Norma Farber First Book Prize. She teaches at St. Mary's College in Moraga, California.

LIBRARY OF CONGRESS CATALOGING-IN-PUBLICATION DATA

Hillman, Brenda.

Loose sugar / Brenda Hillman.

   p.   cm.—(Wesleyan poetry)

ISBN 0–8195–2242–2 (cl. : alk. paper). — ISBN 0–8195–2243–0 (pa. : alk. paper)

I. Title. II. Series.

PS3558.I4526L66   1997

811'.54—dc21   96–44572